The proceeds of this book are donated to the Monks of Saint Benedicts Abbey in Atchison, Kansas

For more ideas on Leadership, Coaching and Culture and the UB4ME Foundation: www.Keithhertling.com

LIFE LESSONS

ON LEADERSHIP COACHING AND CULTURE

KEITH HERTLING

LIFE LESSONS ON LEADERSHIP, COACHING, AND CULTURE

Scripture quotations marked NASB are taken from the New American Standard Bible®, Copyright © 1960, 1962, 1963, 1968, 1971, 1972, 1973, 1975, 1977, 1995 by The Lockman Foundation. Used by permission.

Scripture quotations marked NIV are taken from the Holy Bible, New International Version®. NIV®. Copyright © 1973, 1978, 1984 by International Bible Society. Used by permission of Zondervan. All rights reserved. [Biblica]

iUniverse books may be ordered through booksellers or by contacting:

iUniverse
1663 Liberty Drive
Bloomington, IN 47403
www.iuniverse.com
1-800-Authors (1-800-288-4677)

Because of the dynamic nature of the Internet, any web addresses or links contained in this book may have changed since publication and may no longer be valid. The views expressed in this work are solely those of the author and do not necessarily reflect the views of the publisher, and the publisher hereby disclaims any responsibility for them.

Any people depicted in stock imagery provided by Getty Images are models, and such images are being used for illustrative purposes only.
Certain stock imagery © Getty Images.

ISBN: 978-1-5320-4827-2 (sc)
ISBN: 978-1-5320-4829-6 (hc)
ISBN: 978-1-5320-4828-9 (e)

Library of Congress Control Number: 2018905895

Print information available on the last page.

iUniverse rev. date: 05/24/2018

ABOUT THE AUTHOR

At age fifteen, Keith Hertling embraced entrepreneurship. Somehow, he convinced his mother to convert their two-car garage into what became a local haven for focused athletes, police officers, fireman, and lifeguards. Popeye's Gym was born. It laid the foundation for his future leadership and team-building skills. The fruits of his early success led to his induction into his high school hall of fame in 1996.

His first coaching job was with the Special Olympics, where he would also serve as area director for three years before graduating Benedictine College in Atchison, Kansas, in 1979 with a degree in special education and a minor in theology. He also worked in campus ministry. A three time All-American in football and academics, Keith was inducted into the college's hall of fame in 1994.

A master's degree in counseling education from Kansas University has benefited him throughout his career. He taught and coached football at the junior high, high school, and college level, and he was also a leader in the fitness industry for twenty years as owner and operator of Popeye's Cardio Fitness Center in Topeka, Kansas. His team won many industry awards for innovation and design, and he trademarked *RYTHMETRICS*, a circuit weight-training program structured around music.

Known for his motivational tactics, Keith has been a sought-after certified personal trainer and life coach. During this time, he was awarded a special contract with the Menninger Foundation and enjoyed coaching dozens of NFL and other professional athletes. He was also a program coach for the

American Diabetes Association and led teams in marathon races around the world.

His mission still today is to make you a better version of yourself. His unique skill set is also utilized in coaching franchisees and their managers for Jersey Mike's Subs, as well as mentoring the company's corporate field team to cultivate a culture known as "a sub above."

▌CONTENTS

PLAY TILL THE WHISTLE BLOWS

The summer of '69 was a big one for any twelve-year-old living at the Jersey Shore. But I wasn't just any twelve-year-old—I was a football player. The Golden Elks of Point Pleasant Beach, New Jersey, was my team, and Rod Smith was my coach. Mr. Smith wasn't just any coach either. He was a banker and a golfer, too, and pretty good at both. His modesty would prevent him from bragging that he can shoot his age today at eighty-two. I also met Peter Cancro for the first time on that team, and we would enjoy a unique lifetime friendship. In five short years, he would buy the sub shop he worked at and eventually create a dynasty.

Football was teaching us how to be tough, and somehow this sport gets in your blood at an early age. Sweat, blood, and pain are just a few of the memories that stay alive through the years, but nothing compares to the friendships and camaraderie that are forged on the gridiron. We were learning about teamwork, pushing our limits, caring about the teammates next to us, and running so hard sometimes that we threw up.

I'm sure most of us who practiced and played never really appreciated how good a coach Mr. Smith was. He was a calm soul. Never screamed at us, but he got his point across. Never hit us or hurt us. It seemed like he really cared about us. I'm sure he loved all of us. We learned you could be motivated without getting demeaned. Leaders are demanding, not demeaning.

Coach Smith did like to blow his whistle. One day he blew it so hard at me my ears rang for days. He looked me in the eye and said, "Son, you've got to play till the whistle blows." *That* got my attention, and on that day I began my new journey. That moment changed my life, because from that moment until now, I *have* played till the whistle blows.

Even at twelve years old, I understood I had to finish the play, every play, relentlessly. One of our coaches affectionately referred to some of us as "whirling dervishes"—an endearing term for an energetic, bouncy person who never lets up. The average football play lasts four to five seconds. It doesn't seem like a long time, and yet many players never catch on. You have to complete the job. A champion learns how to get the job done by giving 100 percent effort on every play. This philosophy has followed me through life, and I've learned to apply it to sports, business, and family life.

COACHING ROLE MODELS

Rod Smith was an excellent role model, and his legacy continues today at the Jersey Shore. He taught us that working hard pays dividends. After all, he was a banker. He encouraged us even when we made mistakes. It's not surprising that he would become famous for lending Peter Cancro the money to buy Mike's Subs in 1975 ... but we'll get to that later. It was Rod's excellent example that showed his players how to act. Later in our lives, these early impressions would become the foundation of our coaching, teaching, and parenting philosophies.

Rod's record speaks for itself. Our team was undefeated for three years, and we actually played the top Florida team in the Lunar Bowl in Titusville, Florida, in 1969 and won! What a great experience for young kids. Rod taught us how to win—and furthermore, how to act like champions. Later in my career, I would work with Bill Walsh, coach of the San Francisco 49ers, when they won the Super Bowl in 1985. One of his oft-used phrases was "Posture predicts performance." The way you walk, simply carrying yourself in public, matters. He taught that body language is vital and people look up to leaders.

Point Pleasant Beach High School had a rich tradition in football. Point Pleasant was a small town with a big community of fans and followers. One of our most notable freshman coaches was Steve Jerolaman. Steve was an ex-marine, and he drilled us hard. He treated everyone fairly, and we loved him. He also became the founder and leader of our Adventure Club, which was legendary at the school. Under his leadership, we were undefeated in football, and we were learning how to become leaders. To this day, Steve and Cathy, his wife of fifty years, still live locally and frequent the Garnet Gulls football games.

Our high school role models were also exceptional. Most memorable were Jack White and Don Fioretti, the latter of whom the football field is named after today. By the time senior year came around, we had the makings of a great team. Our fans would say, "They may be slow, but they're small." Maybe we were *physically* small, but we had big hearts. The joke was usually on our opponents, who didn't know that we were also smart. Several of us went on to become leaders on our college campuses and beyond.

Chris Gagnon, for one, graduated magna cum laude from West Point. Richard "Bubba" Bates would go on to play championship rugby and start a multi-million-dollar company in South Carolina. As an offensive guard, he was 160 pounds of twisted steel and sex appeal. Chip Sherman and Mike Spiegel both became teachers and coaches, for thirty-five years each. Combined, they influenced an estimated one hundred thousand kids during their respective careers. Both are in their colleges' hall of fame, and recently Chip was inducted into the Missouri Sports Hall of Fame.

And then there's Peter Cancro. How does a seventeen-year-old high school senior buy a hole-in-the-wall sub shop and turn it into an international award-winning brand (Jersey Mike's Subs, d/b/a Jersey Mike's Franchise Systems)? None of this happens without Rod Smith. I still get a chuckle when Rod tells the story of his bank team questioning his decision to lend a high school kid the equivalent of approximately $1 million today. His answer always is "I knew he would get the ball over the line." Just another sports metaphor. If it was fourth down and one yard to go, give it to Peter because you knew he'd get that yard every time. He knew how to play till the whistle blows, and Rod was his first teacher, coach, banker, and mentor.

These legacies began at an early age and are a testimony to the coaches who we all looked up to. Everyone played both ways, and we were also known for our mental toughness. Jack and Don were no-nonsense fellows and taught us the basics well. They were Vince Lombardi disciples, and our offense became a basic, no-frills, up-the-middle smash-mouth machine. Peter and I were the running backs. We used to fight over who would get the ball in the fourth quarter, because we knew fatigue was setting in on our opponents from us wearing them down. One of us would usually "break a long one" toward the end of the game.

As it turned out, Peter and I were the only ones on the team who would earn scholarships to play in college, and fate would have it that Peter would never go, opting instead to buy the sub shop he'd worked in since the age of fourteen and change the world of sub sandwiches forever. One thing was for sure: we were both well prepared to tackle the world by the coaches who raised us eager to make a difference in the world. We are ever grateful to those coaches, their families, and the community that helped form our character.

The American Legion of New Jersey, like many other states, has sponsored a program since 1946 known as Boys State. It's a weeklong leadership camp for one thousand top-notch elected high school students. It was a prophetic gesture, no doubt, that Peter and I were the two chosen from Point Pleasant Beach High. It would validate our early leadership and entrepreneurial talents. Teams were organically created and tackled projects like building a shed, solving math problems, scheming to capture another team's flag, and competing in water polo. The most significant memory for me was almost drowning in the pool. Apparently, the only side you are allowed to touch is the bottom, where I spent a good bit of time. This experience would launch us into the next phase of our future.

DIVINE PROVIDENCE, POPEYE'S, AND POPE YES

We didn't know it yet, but both Peter and I were about to learn about divine providence—are you where you belong? When Peter had that gut feeling not to go to college but to stay and buy the sub shop, I believe that was the work of the Holy Spirit. He was destined to become what he became and is today. He was at a crossroads, and his inner voice led him to what would eventually become a billion-dollar business.

In 1971, my friends Jerry Kallman, Chuck Waldron, and I formed a club, and Popeye's Gym was born (see picture). It would become part of our legacy. We all wanted scholarships to play football in college, and the recruiters were telling us we were too small, too slow, and too weak. I can recall asking the recruiter what I could do to earn a scholarship, and he said, "Lift weights, do push-ups, and run forties."

Our two-car garage at 618 Atlantic Avenue was quickly converted, with Mom's permission, into a cult gym that would actually produce several college football standouts; Jeff King, a Mr. Universe; Chuck Waldron, a Mr. America; and a professional wrestler by the name of Page Falkinburg, a.k.a. Diamond Dallas Page, who would become the WWF world champion. Page had a storybook career. His book *Positively*

Page chronicles his life on and off the stage (or in this case, wrestling mat). His philanthropy continues today as he helps resurrect older and less fortunate wrestling brothers. You can find out about his internationally popular DDP Yoga program at www.diamonddallaspage.com.

Most of us were Davids and not Goliaths. The recruiter never told us how many or how much we should do. Our relentless attitude and mind-set led us to what Malcolm Gladwell refers to as the "10,000 hours" concept in his book *Outliers* (www.blinkist.com). Most great performances take a tremendous amount of effort and practice, whether athletic, musical, or tactical. The really great ones, like Olympic athletes, make it look easy. Most forget how difficult and time-consuming the journey is to the top.

Over the next few years, we ran thousands of forties, lifted weights for hundreds of hours, and could do every and any type of push-up that ever existed. We ate, drank, slept, and even dreamed about our workouts, and all those hours would pay off. We were learning how to become leaders and coaches by example and by deed. Our brothers would eventually take over the gym as the original gang became college-bound, heading for their proverbial glories.

It was the summer of '75. Peter now owned the shop and was working all day seven days a week. No fun at the beach, no fooling around. His work ethic would become the standard for any new hire, and what happened behind the counter defined the success that Jersey Mike's would become. He took the shop to a whole new level. It became the Cheers of our town and a welcome warm genuine smile was always available any time of the day. It was the go-to destination for all sub lovers, and in the summertime that meant lines way out the door.

I loved my hometown, but I was off to play football in

California … only I would never arrive there. That's where divine providence comes in for me.

The plan was to drive across country and drop my friend Tom Spiegel off at Benedictine College in Atchison, Kansas, and then head west. We arrived for the first time on campus in the dark. As we drove up a steep hill leading to what we would learn was a monastery, we accidently ran into a black-robed monk. Fortunately, he wasn't hurt, but he looked up from the ground at my personalized Popeye's license plate and remarked, "Son, I like your tag: Pope Yes!" We later learned that Brother John was a fairly new monk, and we would both remember this moment for years to come. He still wanders the campus spreading joy and blessings to all he meets.

That was the moment. I didn't get much sleep that night. The football coach saw me at breakfast and may have hypnotized me, because I never left. Call it divine providence. The pope himself said, "If you are where you truly belong and nourish your brother and sister, you will flourish." I didn't know it yet, but I was definitely in the right place. It would become a very special place for me the rest of my life. Saint Benedict once said, "Bloom where you are planted." That's an interesting thought, especially if you move around a lot, as the coaching profession would require.

I was about to become the beneficiary of not one but three hall-of-fame coaches. Talk about role models! Coach George Tardiff became a great mentor and friend. Years later, I would become his defensive coordinator at Washburn University, and we would win a conference championship. Daryl Jones was the head basketball coach and helped George as an assistant. He cared enough about me that when he heard I might not return after my freshman year, he flew to New Jersey to give me counsel. That's the definition of caring, and this man made it cool to care. He played on a national championship team and became an All-American and NAIA Hall of Famer. Larry Wilcox, also an assistant, would become head football coach after George for the next forty years (and currently) and was inducted into the NAIA Hall of Fame in 2016. His entire life from that point was as a servant leader coach and teacher. He practically single-handedly reinvented the program and brought it to national prominence.

All three of these special men possessed the leadership skills of humility, compassion, and listening. Love, serve, care—they taught us through example, and they taught us the habits would stick with us for a lifetime. All three had graduated from Saint Benedict's, as it was known before changing its name to Benedictine in 1970. All three were members of a secret, esoteric "cult" that I would soon benefit from.

MONKS AND MENTORS

Walk with the wise and become wise but
collaborate with fools and fare badly.
—Proverbs 13:2

If you every want to learn humility, walk with a monk for an hour. Maybe a day? Success is in the way you walk the paths of life. I lived in and around the monastic community for eight years. "The boys," as I affectionately referred to them, had a profound and amazing effect on my life and helped shape the teacher, coach, man, and father I would become.

If you want to learn leadership, study under someone monk-like. Find a mentor who has life skills. The monks' life was the ultimate example of service to God, of course, but also service to community and service to their fellow monks and men.

Ora et labora is Latin for "pray and work." All the monks believed that work was a form of prayer. It was a rule of Saint Benedict. It helps lead to happiness. Saint Augustine said, "Holiness creates happiness." After all, isn't happiness the number one human desire?

Let me tell you what happiness is not: practicing football in hundred-degree heat three times a day and no air-conditioning in the dorm. We were all told we were building character. Maybe so, but I quickly learned college football was a lot different from high school.

Everybody knows that sports in general develops discipline and leadership. In high school, captains were picked based on what the coach saw. In college, the team *voted* on the captains. Generally, it was the quiet leader, one who easily encouraged and inspired others, who would become the captain of the team. This was the guy who looked after others, the one who took the last shower and who made sure everybody was on the bus. That guy was Johnny Clark, and although he was only three years older, he also became a mentor to me. I looked up to him and wanted to learn. He was a model team leader, and by definition he would have his followers. After all, you can call yourself a leader, but without followers, you're just a team captain assigned by the coach.

Saint Benedict's Monastery was built in 1857 on the historic Missouri River bluffs—one of the highest and most beautiful locations in Kansas, with breathtaking views. Saint Benedict's College opened the following year. Football as a sport was once a rich tradition, but hard times in the fifties and sixties led the abbot (head monk) to drop the sport in 1962. It would be reinstated in 1970, and fielding a new team was no easy task.

George Tardiff was hired as coach. He was a member of the 1958 national championship team and the perfect guy for the job. He convinced me at that fateful breakfast to join the Ravens. He was quite the salesman, and he was quite the coach. "Don't be a small fish in a big pond, son—here you can be a big fish in a little pond," he said, and it sounded good to me.

And he was right. Although an all-state player in New Jersey, I was untested in college, and everyone but me thought I was undersized. But it was in my sophomore year that life would forever change and my career path would be clear.

In his heart man plans his course but
the Lord directs his footsteps.
—Proverbs 16:9

Influence is the word that describes one of my favorite pictures that hangs in my office today: it shows a small boy standing alone looking at a group of bigger boys sitting in a circle. How does a monk influence your life? I can recall an occasion when I got in a little trouble off-campus. My monk mentor Father Dennis asked me if I realized how many people were looking up to me and how my success on and off the field could influence others. He asked me if I knew the tremendous impact I could have on others. His message was that my thoughts, words, and actions mattered—and not just for me but for everyone around me.

Light bulb! His question led me to some serious reflection. I knew I could be a better leader, and so I decided to exhibit humility on the football field. Every time I scored a touchdown, instead of spiking the ball, I would take a knee, bless myself, and point to heaven. This little gesture almost immediately was adopted by my teammates and became our standard "touchdown dance."

The power of example should be in the toolbox of every coach/teacher who is cultivating moral leadership. Forty years later, the fans still remember the team from 1976 that won the bowl game and took a knee for every touchdown.

My first monk mentor gave me insight into the following:

- my role
- my goal
- my soul

What did I want to be, what did I want to accomplish, and did I want to bring my soul with me? I've used this same simple format with my players, staff, and clients over the years.

The most powerful leadership tool you
have is your own personal example.

—John Wooden

In 1976, the Ravens of Benedictine were invited to play
Washburn University in the Boot Hill Bowl in Dodge City,
Kansas. Our team motto that year was "You gotta believe,"
instilled by Coach Tardiff. Talk about cultivating culture. His
personal example of dedication and will to win gave us the
formula for building a championship team. His hero, Vince
Lombardi, said it best: "Winning is not everything—but
making the effort to win is." It's the will to win that guides
you to the end of the goal. The power of belief makes all the
difference. The champion learns to remove doubt from the
equation.

Today at Jersey Mike's Training Center, you will find one
entire wall covered in words that describe our history. Our
brand manifesto's opening line is "Jersey Mike's is a brand that
believes: in the value of ingredients, in the virtue of intention,
and in the idea that making a sub sandwich and making a
difference can be one and the same." Belief in value. Belief
in virtue. Building a great culture requires getting a team to
believe—in the cause and in each other.

Sports as a metaphor for life is one of the greatest clichés.
We love this at Jersey Mike's mainly because of the team concept
and how it takes a team behind the line to make a great sub
every time, all the time. Slicer, sprinkler, wrapper, register—no
one is more important or more valuable than the other.

That *belief* type of culture motivated a group of small college
misfits restarting a program from scratch. We believed as David
believed when he slew Goliath—and that's who we were playing
in the Boot Hill Bowl, a school seven times bigger than ours. It

didn't matter, because our coach cultivated a winning attitude and, in a short time, banded a group of strangers into a fierce fighting unit that believed in each other and believed they could beat even Goliath (in this case, Washburn University).

Details of the game are well archived, but what isn't is the feeling inside, like David must have felt when the ten-foot giant hit the ground defeated. It's the feeling of how a team believing in something can overcome obstacles like doubt and disbelief. That's what a coach can do. That's what our coach did and all coaches should do and must do to become consistent winners.

THE INTERVIEW

Shortly after that game, my life would change forever. Our local paper, the *Atchison Globe*, asked me for an interview. I guess there was a good reason for an interview, but it wasn't what I was thinking. Micky Parman's agenda became quite clear with her final question: "You know, I think you would make a great coach, and did you know we have an opening?" Wow. I've heard flattery can get you everywhere, but maybe I *could* be a coach and there *is* an opening. Why not? I could use the extra money.

But wait—what am I coaching? My head was spinning, and she had me in the palm of her hand. She was shrewd and cleverly set me up. What could a sophomore in college coach anyway? I was just a jock with a soft heart, and she pounced on me like a lion jumping a gazelle. I was sucked in and had no idea of what was to come.

Turned out it was the local chapter of Special Olympics that needed a coach. The position was volunteer, and I decided to take a shot. No money? No big deal. It would become my first brush with community service and be ever so valuable later when I opened up my own Jersey Mike's and became deeply integrated in the community.

When the bus pulled up for my first day of coaching, I was stunned. There were twelve kids ranging in age from twelve to twenty-two. I was eighteen years old myself with no real coaching experience. I did know a thing or two about weight training, though, and my plan was to use our very basic universal gym on campus and teach some circuits.

Before the bus driver drove away, I asked why one kid had a helmet on. The driver said not to worry—that kid had seizures, but he'd already had his today. The driver then smirked and said, "I'll be back in an hour." It only took Big John, as his teammates called him, a few minutes, and then I was witnessing my first grand mal seizure. Needless to say, it is still ingrained in my memory.

Lisa Gellings, who would become the team captain, assured me John would be okay and the seizure wouldn't last long. Little did I know my relationship with Lisa would last a lifetime. We would eventually get a job placement for Lisa in the college cafeteria, where she would work for over thirty years literally serving her community and contributing to society her entire life.

Before the hour was over, I had fallen in love with my group of "special athletes. I would become their beloved coach and soon accept the area directorship for northeast Kansas and retain that position for three years until graduation. My dream of becoming a lawyer—inspired by my hometown hero, Jack Ford—was over. My new major would be special education. Hook, line, and sinker, I was in—and my studies, especially of learning styles, would prove to be invaluable in my tool chest of coaching.

LEARNING STYLES

Why Can't They Learn It Right?

Meek and mild they sit there staring into space,
Looks of sheer bewilderment, frustration on their face.
I know that they can hear me. I know their ears are good,
But something in between them isn't working as it should.
When will there be a breakthrough?
There must be hope for some.
The child works hard for weeks on end
but progress doesn't come.
These kids are called "retarded," their lives are sealed in fate,
Some never cease to live in fear, some do but always late.
Oh please, please try to help them.
Why can't they learn it right?
Why can't their minds work normally?
Please help them to be bright.
When will we find the answers on how these children live?
When will we finally realize how much they have to give?

Have you ever heard not all kids learn alike? That's especially true of kids with intellectual and developmental disabilities. Some struggle to learn at all. College course work showed me that some are visual learners, some auditory, and some tactile kinesthetic. Many kids were also very uncomfortable if you touched them. Even a simple hug or arm around the back would make them cringe.

A good teacher needs to observe how each kid can learn most effectively. You couldn't teach everyone the same, and this is still true today. Most of us learn in a combination of those three learning styles, but it helps to understand how we learn if we're going to be great teachers and coaches in our workplaces, and especially in our Jersey Mike's restaurants. A typical staff will be multigenerational with a variety of personalities, from millennials to baby boomer, and a great coach will understand the learning cone and make sure to intentionally involve and engage all the team members and find out how each of them learns. Everybody knows we have to coach our people. How are you coaching them?

We need to look for "coaching moments" in our workplaces and especially in our restaurants. We have the research. Edgar Dale's model shows that 90 percent of our learning comes from *doing* the requested task—learning through the experience. We know it's not enough to tell or read or write or combine these styles; we need to coach the experience if we want a great experience for every customer. We need to train our people with the heart of a teacher. Learn how they learn, especially through role-playing and video. All coaches know the value of playing back the film, because film never lies. We have a great responsibility as teachers and coaches to know how each crew member learns. Don't just rely on regional representatives to teach everything. They don't have the same relationship with your crew members as you do.

Learning Pyramid (Edgar Dale)

PerspectiveS for Pharmacy Educators

Excellence

Teaching

Successful

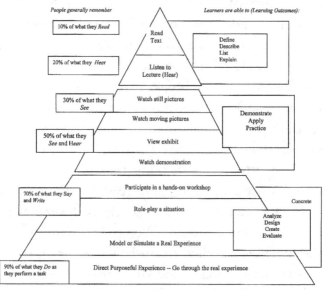

Dale's Cone of Experience

Heidi Milia Anderson, Ph.D.,
Assistant Dean for Education Innovation, University of Kentucky

Description. Dale's Cone of Experience is a model that incorporates several theories related to instructional design and learning processes. During the 1960s, Edgar Dale theorized that learners retain more information by what they "do" as opposed to what is "heard", "read" or "observed". His research led to the development of the Cone of Experience. Today, this "learning by doing" has become known as "experiential learning" or "action learning". The cone is diagramed and explained in the next sections.

Cone of Experience

People generally remember

Learners are able to (Learning Outcomes):

10% of what they *Read*

Read Text

Define
Describe
List
Explain

20% of what they *Hear*

Listen to Lecture (Hear)

30% of what they *See*

Watch still pictures

Watch moving pictures

Demonstrate
Apply
Practice

50% of what they *See* and *Hear*

View exhibit

Watch demonstration

Participate in a hands-on workshop

70% of what they *Say* and *Write*

Concrete

Role-play a situation

Analyze
Design
Create
Evaluate

Model or Simulate a Real Experience

90% of what they *Do* as they perform a task

Direct Purposeful Experience -- Go through the real experience

Source: Adapted from E. Dale, <u>Audiovisual Methods in Teaching</u>, 1969, NY: Dryden Press.

I can still recall my first year as a special education teacher. The setting was a junior high school learning center, where I inherited three amazing veteran paraprofessionals. They were eager to see the new young guy in action.

My love for poetry would soon be transferred to the reports known as the IEP (individualized educational plan). Every student had to have a personal master plan, and this took great planning and getting to know the potential of every kid. When your IQ tested out below 80, you got labeled "mentally retarded." My goal was to get as many as possible above that 80-point standard. Many kids were borderline and just fell behind because of a poor home life and other extenuating circumstances. Once you got that label, it was hard to shake.

When I presented my first poetry lesson, my staff laughed at me and predicted that this would be a futile exercise because it was way above the scope of these kids. Some had reading levels that were several years behind. Others could barely read at all. The kids, however, liked the idea when I pitched it. It wasn't long before Harry Fafafnick, with a little help, came up with his poem:

> In everything you do and say
> in everything about your way
> from the morning till the end of day,
> You are your attitude.
> —Harry Fafafnick, eighth-grade special-education class, 1980

My para staff was right: most all the kids struggled with the poem concept and never really caught on. But one did! And that one put me on a mission. My purpose was apparent, and I was on my way to becoming a great coach and teacher. This little guy inspired me to create my very first mission statement, which I still carry today:

> Wake up and choose an attitude of gratitude. Be intentional with every task that comes across my desk and ask God to help me make a difference in somebody's life today.

Harry set me on a mission, and you can't be on a mission without a mission statement. Attitude is everything, and gratitude changes everything. Science teaches us that being grateful inspires chemical changes in the body. Everybody knows you can't be thankful and worried at the same time. A good coach learns to develop a heart of gratitude—and a great coach, after he learns it himself, will then teach it.

I took my personal mission statement seriously. I recall an exercise several years later, when I was in the fitness business. Upon opening our first center, I took my team to a weekend workshop with Thomas Plummer to design our own company statement. We actually spent hours debating, discussing, and even arguing about what we wanted it to say about us.

This investment in my staff proved invaluable. They created their own mission and bought in. To this day, I can recite the words we inscribed on plexiglass and hung over our main lobby to welcome all who entered our sanctuary:

> Show up and we'll show you a personalized fitness program, individual custom and ongoing training in an atmosphere created to guide YOU to accomplishing YOUR goals and dreams.

My team believed in this mission. That core group stayed together for nearly twenty years. If you want to cultivate great culture, don't give your team a mission statement; rather, spend the time teaching them to design it themselves with your coaching. What a great way to take ownership! The staff will surely believe in something they helped create. Success is in the little things.

At Jersey Mike's headquarters in Manasquan, New Jersey, you will see in the entryway of our main building the simple mission statement Peter created way back in 1975:

Giving. Make a difference in someone's life.

He's been doing that for a lifetime, and last I checked, it's working. Whenever I see our old coach Rod Smith, he wants to know how many stores have been opened so he can calculate how many jobs can be attributed to Peter. Obviously, it's a big number and a part of Peter's legacy that continues to grow.

There is a coach's creed by Edward Everett Hale:

I am only one but I am one. I can't do everything but I can do something. That which I can I ought to do and by the grace of God, I shall.

This creed immediately spoke to me. I heard that one man *can* make a difference. I was formulating what "a sub above" would mean to me years later by applying these concepts with Jersey Mike's.

I was on fire with my passion for coaching. I would surround myself with books, audiotapes and videos and get to every conference possible. I would start with the biggest conference available. It was my great fortune to work at several medalist clinics, driving the top coaches in the country to and from airports. Imagine a young coach getting one-on-one attention from the best in the business. My coaching gurus are too many to list, but this awesome experience solidified my calling as *coach*.

Save one, save the world—that's what my grandmother would say. After finding the coach's creed, I knew what I had to do next: get to the National Coaches Convention. It was only my first year as a junior high teacher and football coach (my stipend in 1979 was $300), but I knew I had the coaching bug and would be at the high school level next. I decided I was heading to the conference in Houston over winter break.

As fate would have it, my Jeep broke down on the way, but I learned from my training with the monks and turned that setback into a comeback. After a day's hitchhiking, I would make it to see the keynote speaker, nationally renowned coach Bear Bryant from Alabama. It was all worth it, and I learned more about culture and coaching in one week than all my previous experience.

Success is in the little things you do and in the things you say.

OUR CULTURE

What is culture, and how does a coach cultivate it? It's your attitude and the way you think. It's buying into the way we operate. It's what we believe in, and it becomes a way of life.

Here's an example: In 1978, Peter decided it was time to come out to Kansas and see his buddy play football in person. When we picked him up at the airport, he had two suitcases: one for his clothes and one stuffed full of products and materials to set up a sub shop right there on the premises in the Kansas City airport. Imagine Peter borrowing a table from maintenance and preparing the sub line, complete with all the fixings for a dozen delicious subs personally and authentically made by him to feed his friends and family. That's servant leadership in a nutshell. He went way out of his way to make life better for others.

That gives you a glimpse of what culture is and can be. At Jersey Mike's, we say, "Great culture attracts great people. People are our purpose, and leaders take care of their people." Culture can help companies retain workers, which can give them an edge in our industry where turnover is 110 percent, according to Sullivan.com.

So many books have been written on coaching, culture, and leadership. One of my favorites is *Leaders Eat Last* by Simon Sinek. He's a big believer in the bottom-up leadership we know as servant leadership. Essentially, it means putting others first. Somewhere along my studies with the monks, I recall something about the first shall be last and the last shall be first. I think Simon figured out that this philosophy works in life and in business.

Every great leader has a selfless quality—the mind-set of *I am second.* That is putting others first. I also love the FAMILY foundation, an acronym for Forget about Me I Love You. We apply this principle every chance we get.

> Life's most persistent and urgent question
> is, "What are you doing for others?"
> —Martin Luther King

C. S. Lewis would call this humility, and he defines it in this way: "Humility is not thinking less of myself, humility is thinking of myself less." Learn to put yourself on the shelf and put others first. That is how you cultivate culture. At Jersey Mike's, our franchisees and managers know they have two families, and the family-first philosophy is important. It's hard to separate the home family from the work family. In fact, there is a terrific TED Talk series that speaks to this issue (Dr. Bahira Sharif Trask and Nigel Marsh, ted.com/talks).

In his book *The Culture Engine*, author Chris Edmonds says that "Culture drives everything that happens in an organization each day." He suggests looking at a company's culture through the eyes of the customer. Our training department has been teaching this for years and declares this is how we get the unvarnished truth. Ultimately, it's the customer who decides if we are a sub above. I think it's clear that we can't leave our culture to chance.

> Culture has to really be owned by the leadership, but it also has to happen in every layer of an organization.
> —Laine Joelson Cohen

I opened up my first Jersey Mike's franchise in Topeka, Kansas, in the winter of 2003. As a franchisee, I was in charge of leadership, culture, and coaching. My staff was well trained, and our opening week was huge. The following week, I received an unexpected visit from Father Barnabas, the abbot of the Benedictine monastery and my first monk mentor. He sat and observed the entire lunch rush. Afterward, I sat with him as he ate his regular—number 7, Mike's Way. I'll always remember his words: "Keith, what a great ministry you have here."

He saw the connections with the customers, the engagement of the crew with each other, and the synergy that we hope we get with a well-coached team. I took his words to heart and, upon reflection, started to see my sub shop as more than just a sub shop. It could be my church, and it became a more sacred place to me.

I shared this vision with my manager and the team, and we began to cultivate a culture that everyone who came into our domain would be treated like a saint. That visit from the abbot was an epiphany, and our purpose would change the way we worked. It reaffirmed my personal commitment to become a better version of myself every day.

> Anyone can be a great player but not everyone can be a great teammate.
> —Coach Mike Krzyzewski

At Jersey Mike's we like sports metaphors—especially those pertaining to football—because of one basic thing: teamwork. Developing team culture needs to be intentional. We love to get involved in competitions, such as the Tough Mudder, that inspire mental and physical toughness. In addition, competing with a team can help an individual attain a goal that would never be accomplished alone. (See photo of the Mudders.)

We need managers to learn how to coach and cultivate a culture. Without that, life is a lot harder at home and in the workplace. We love relating to football because of the unique diversity in players' positions, talents, and sizes. We like to recruit athletes because they understand working together as a team and the sense of urgency. They can move! We love to huddle up before a lunch rush and get motivated as a team to put on our show.

"Follow-up and follow-through equal no fumbles." You will hear this phrase used often at our Jersey Mike's team meetings. Another sports metaphor, but it's true, and a great strategy in our day and age of emails, texts, and other impersonal forms of communication that can be missed or misconstrued. Follow-up and follow-through for us usually involve the phone—good old-fashioned talking on the phone so there can be no miscommunication, or fumbles. In the game of football, a fumble could mean losing the game. In the game of life, even one fumble can mean losing a relationship, losing a contract, or losing a lot of money. Sometimes picking up the phone to follow up on one of our modern-day messages can prevent a catastrophe.

During our phase 2 leadership school, we spend some serious time on an important assignment. It's a one-pager, and it's like a sacred scroll for us. It really embodies a large piece of our culture all wrapped up into two hundred words. The words matter—words like *virtue, always, value, give, elevate, extra,* and *unexpected.* Our students will pick out the words that speak to them and discuss what they mean.

It's one of my favorite sessions, and I always enjoy the way Coach Hughes teaches it. It's never the same twice. Just like a coach recruits players for the team, employees must fit into our culture before they get signed by the team. The first thing they have to do is watch a 2:36 video that embodies our culture. We call it our manifesto.

JERSEY MIKE'S BRAND MANIFESTO

Jersey Mike's is a brand that believes: In the value of ingredients, in the virtue of intention, and in the idea that making a sub sandwich and making a difference can be one and the same.

At Jersey Mike's, we offer a sub above – one that's measured in more than inches or seconds 'til served. We carefully consider every aspect of what we do – every slice, every sandwich, every store – we provide our customers with sustenance and substance too.

We start with a strong foundation: the kind of high-grade ingredients you'd use yourself if you could. Premium meats sliced on the spot, the freshest vegetables... a hot grill always ready and delectable bread baked throughout the day. And then...there's the juice. Red wine vinegar and olive oil.

The juice. It's what turns good into great, better into best, and it elevates our sandwich to the highest level. The juice is the active ingredient in a sub above. It's an exquisite zing... a splash of extra and unexpected.

Of course the concept goes beyond sandwiches: Life is better with juice too. **A little added effort, a splash of extra and unexpected, elevates everything.** So we take the time to know your name. We enliven where we can. And when we ask "how can we help?" we mean it.

After all, helping is who we are. It's not an angle and it's not an act. We don't give to get, we give to give: Our passion, our time, our talent, and our attention...we always have and always will.

We believe staying true to your roots is critical. Your history, after all, is a running start for your future. The key to authenticity is this: Remember where you came from, remember where you're going, and choose the straightest line between the two.

If you're good, be good always.
If you're true, be true always.

And if you're the best submarine sandwich on the planet,
be the best submarine sandwich on the planet always.

Jersey Mike's.
Help nourish. Help flourish. Be a sub above.

The manifesto was created by Planet Propaganda, a third-party advertising company. They interviewed dozens of the company's staff, customers, and officers. This version was their first attempt. Peter loved it and said, "Thanks. We'll take it as is." It really does sum up our culture, and our new recruits see who we are right away. If they get goose bumps after they watch the video, they're going to get hired!

We teach not to hire on the first interview. We have replaced the word *hire* with *recruit*. We are recruiting a team with the intent of making a championship run. You won't win without good players. We are recruiting the best for each position as they try out for the team—always building the bench.

Another vehicle we use to cultivate culture is a video series we call "56 Seconds of Sub-Above Culture." It's another example of the monks' influence. The Benedictines produce a weekly one-minute videos of a relevant church message, short and to the point. This inspired us to make ours fifty-six seconds (1956 being the year Mike's was established). Our messages are short and sweet, and the Jersey Mike's managers have a consistent way of teaching culture to our frontline employees.

Most of our managers across the country attend our leadership school at our original store, which has been converted into a training center. It's a special time for our home leadership team to welcome and bond with our newest "soldiers." Hallowed ground for sure to see the original sub shop where Peter and his early teams would sell upward of a thousand subs a day in the summer. Before our students leave, they are "baptized" in the spirit of Jersey Mike's.

Probably the most fun event under our Cultivating Culture menu is our National G13 Competition, originally created by Danny Malamis and Team Washington for our DC region. Our training and ops team now lead a nationwide contest. How fast can we make a perfect giant number 13—the Original Italian with six meats from our menu? Proper weight and proper procedures, just how we make a beautiful sub sandwich every day. On a typical day at Jersey Mike's, we will sell more than fourteen thousand.

Judges look to the final product. We need to see a great sub created with great urgency. This event epitomizes coaching the basics. Fundamentals first. "Slow down to move faster." Every store in every market gets a chance to compete for the trophy at our national convention. We invest in our people, and it pays off every day at the store level.

Another important piece of our culture is our store openings. Passing out ten thousand free coupons may seem counterintuitive, but it's how we invite our communities to try us out. It's Peter's principle 7 that he established more than forty years ago. If done correctly, it works wonderfully. We make our store openings a great festive event. An amazing team effort is needed, and one valuable player is our Mike's Concierge.

Our free coupons are redeemed in the first five days, and the lines are out the door. A presence in the lobby is the perfect way to make the first impression. The personality of the Mike's Concierge reflects the store's image and energy. In fact, most stores will have two on duty all day for ten days, knowing the value in greeting our future valuable customers, showing them how to order, answering and explaining our culture, and talking about the charity that will benefit from their visit. The Mike's Concierge is usually the franchisee, a corporate office representative, or a team member with great personality and enthusiasm. I personally have helped dozens of stores and after several days can be exhausted, but the value of making a new customer is always exciting and rewarding.

After the dust settles following an opening, our stores are up and running successfully with the expert market plan our office provides. But it all starts with every store personally inviting surrounding businesses and neighbors with a free sub where a local charity will benefit. It's Stephen Covey's fourth habit of highly successful people: "Think win-win."

Probably the most unique of our cultural concepts is our Month of Giving and our Day of Giving. Every potential new franchisee who is looking to join our team is introduced to what has been, I believe, a key to our overall success. Every store picks its own local charity in March that will benefit from 100 percent of the sales from the designated day and also funds from the entire month. We get 100 percent buy-in because it works.

Peter didn't invent cause marketing, but he's been doing it since he bought the shop in 1975. Today, it translates into a great thing for all our communities. This year, our store in Olathe, Kansas, donated the most money in the country to its local charity, Braden's Hope. The one-day take was over $20,000. That's over 1,000 subs in one day. Many stores throughout the country were close behind. Every year, our company's totals exceed the previous year, and it's in the millions. Connecting with our communities is an integral piece of who we are. As our manifesto states, "We give to give."

One of the intriguing cultures I've followed over the years is the team of the New Zealand Blacks. Their history of success clearly reflects the amazing culture they have designed and passed down through the years. They are a feared organization all over the world, and here are a few of their core principles:

1. *Sweep the sheds.* Before leaving the dressing room at the end of the game, some of the most famous names in world rugby stop and tidy up after themselves. They literally

and figuratively sweep the sheds. Though it might seem strange for a team of imperious dominance, humility is central to their culture. The All Blacks believe that it's impossible to achieve stratospheric success without having your feet planted firmly on the ground.

2. *Follow the spearhead.* In Maori, *whanau* means "extended family." It's symbolized by the spearhead. Though a spearhead has three tips, to be effective, all its force must move in one direction. Not a single part of the spearhead should deviate from what bonds the team together. The All Blacks select on character as well as talent, which means that a number of prominent young players in New Zealand never get selected.

3. *Champions do extra.* Former All Black Brad Thorn's mantra, "Champions do extra," helped him become one of the single most successful players in rugby history. The philosophy simply means finding incremental ways to do more: in the gym, on the field, or for the team. It is much like the philosophy of marginal gains used by Team Sky. A focus on continual improvement, the creation of a continual learning environment, and a willingness to spill blood for the jersey was at the core of Graham Henry's All Black culture.

Understanding these responsibilities creates a compelling sense of higher purpose. It's a good lesson for us all: if we play a bigger game, we play a more effective game. Better people make better All Blacks—but they also make better doctors and lawyers, bankers and businessmen, fathers, brothers, and friends.

BE A SUB ABOVE

"A champion is never fully satisfied." That was the statement painted above the door of our football stadium in college. Every man would smack it on his way out to the battlefield.

Years later, as we cultivated our culture at Jersey Mike's, this memory came back to me. It's part of what "a sub above" is all about. Is it the sub? Is it the people? The experience? When we travel the country on our Sub Above tour, many of our crew members chime in and give us their thoughts. This is what they tell us:

- It's in the loving of our customers, and they love coming to work.
- It's in taking great pride in serving a great product.
- It's the genuine banter with every guest.

A sub above puts you in a higher position, a higher purpose. That's how you build a champion, and that's when we break out Peter's seven principles. Peter was developing his leadership skills at hyper-speed even at a young age. He learned from the older guys around him who valued his opinion. He came up with his "7 Principles of Success" that we still use today.

7 PRINCIPLES *of* SUCCESS

1 **Is my restaurant clean and well maintained?** This seems almost too simple, but I know (and our research bears this out) that customers expect a clean store. A store that does not sparkle disappoints customers. Disappointed customers do not return.

2 **Is my restaurant well stocked?** Properly stocked meat cases and chip racks show that the owner and manager care. Customers like that.

3 **Are my products fresh?** We pride ourselves on making the freshest, most flavorful sandwiches in the business. That's why our onions, lettuce and tomatoes must always be the absolute freshest and best they can. There are many restaurants that serve average food at lower prices. If we want to beat them, our food has to be fresher.

4 **Are all my team members neat and well groomed?** Serving food to customers is a big responsibility. Our team must inspire confidence in our customers. Clean uniforms and good grooming are necessary to inspire the trust of our customers.

5 **Are we making the subs with proper procedures?** Our success depends on the consistent execution of sub making. If we follow our procedures, we will serve an excellent sandwich. If we do not, we give up our best chance to wow the customer.

6 **Are we sharing our lives with our customers?** Our customers are important to us - treat them that way. Our business is much more than just serving a product; it involves establishing a personal relationship with the people who buy our sandwiches. Make friends with your customers.

These first six questions will help you build the foundation of your success. Until you can answer each of them with unequivocal, "Yes!" you will not be successful in our business. Once you have the foundation in place, you can ask yourself the last question.

7 **Have I invited people into my restaurant?** Even the cleanest and best-operated restaurant will fail if no one knows about it. Once you have mastered the first six questions, proudly ask people into your restaurant. You have to ask for the sale.

Help nourish. Help flourish.
BE A SUB ABOVE.

EVERYTHING STARTS WITH THE HEART

---❖---

The Best Way

Many times I've written, and many times I've said,
The best way we can show our love is to live the life He led.
The best way we can show we care,
living His example everywhere.
The best way we can show our love is to
let the heart control the head.
We can memorize our lessons, we can
teach the things He did;
These things are good, but we also
should live the life He lived.
We can learn to share, to show we care,
But the best gift we could ever give is to
live your life as He would live.
We can talk about the healings and tell about His deeds,
We can share together much in prayer
how He fulfills our needs,
But the best thing we could every do is
to love the way He'd want us to.

---❖---

Success is being big of heart; it's not something measured by our peers. I once heard a coach describe a player as having a "heart as big as this room." At Jersey Mike's, we teach all our field personnel to develop the heart of a teacher and the heart of a coach.

> With all vigilance guard your heart—
> for in it is the source of all life.
> —Proverbs 4:23

The monks used to say that if your heart's not right, your words won't be right. What you say reveals what's in your heart, and words are a two-edged sword. Words can inspire. They can motivate. They can cultivate and elevate. They empower us. But they can also demean. They can devastate. They can deflate. They can anger. They can demoralize. Once they come out, like toothpaste from a tube, they can't go back in and are very hard to reconcile.

The heart of a coach helps you choose words wisely and know it's not just the message but *how* it's delivered. Words matter. They create your world. Your words create your world, and it all starts with the heart.

> Wherever you go, go with all your heart.
> —Confucius

We are what we think and then what we say. I believe the quality of your thinking determines the quality of your life. Wisdom and knowledge come from listening, not yapping. Further, words change things: "I forgive you." Words can change the world: "I have a dream." Words tell stories. The greatest story ever told is made up of words written by men but given to them by God—*inspired*. Our Bible, the best-selling book of all time, is a story with inspired words.

And what about words not spoken? "I love you" or "I'm so proud of you" or "Do you know how special you are?" Usually this occurs with our "loved" ones, especially our children, who without these words can develop a lifetime of woes.

> Those that guard mouth and tongue
> guard themselves from trouble.
> —Proverbs 21:23

So, watch what you say. Use your words wisely. They are a reflection of what's in your heart.

> The babble of some people is like sword thrusts,
> but the tongue of the wise is healing.
> —Proverbs 12:18

QUALITIES OF A SUB-ABOVE COACH

———— ❊ ————

The Coach

Books, paper, pencils, pens—some tools the coach uses.
A job that's tough to comprehend and
one which courage chooses.
The many roles which one must fill
with fewer hours to finish,
At time becomes an act of will as energies diminish.
A friend, a foe, most seem to know what gets kids motivated.
Year in, year out, they teach and show
how learning is created.
From day one on, they build upon each
mind to reach potentials,
And hopefully each will respond with highest of credentials.
The coach is responsible for failure and success,
And though most are very capable,
some do succumb to stress.
But the coach stands above the crowd
with character and pride,
Profession of the wise and proud, no learning be denied.

———— ❊ ————

When you break down the word *quality*, you get excellence at something. At Jersey Mike's, our leaders need to possess the following qualities. If they don't, can you coach them up?

ENCOURAGEMENT

> Definition: give support, confidence or hope to someone. Synonyms: hearten, cheer, buoy up, uplift, inspire, motivate, spur on, stir, stir up, fire up, stimulate, invigorate, vitalize, embolden, fortify, rally.

One of my monk mentors in college was Abbot Barnabas ("son of encouragement"). He used to say, "To encourage someone is putting courage into their hearts." Coaching isn't about judging people; it's about encouraging them.

In 1988, the Colorado University football team was playing Nebraska for a shot at the national title. In this game, star running back Eric Bieniemy fumbled the ball three times in the first half. As the teams headed to the locker rooms for halftime, you saw something special from head coach Bill McCartney. He had his arm around Eric, a simple yet powerful motivating gesture that doesn't even require words. Some coaches would have berated or embarrassed their player in this situation, but not Bill. He knew the power of encouragement.

Unbelievably, Eric would fumble again in the third quarter of the game, but in the fourth quarter he rushed for four touchdowns, and the Buffalos won the game. That's still a record to this day, and it was chronicled in the ESPN series *30 for 30*, "The Gospel according to Mac."

How many crew members might benefit from a simple arm

around the shoulder or encouraging word? Don't miss simple opportunities to make a difference.

Bill O'Connor was a member of the 1976 Benedictine Boot Hill Bowl champs. Forty years later, he'd be standing on the field during halftime at the homecoming game with his teammates getting inducted into the hall of fame. That's when he asked me if I remembered the chat we had forty years earlier in the locker room where Bill decided he would call it quits after a rough practice. I saw him sitting with his head down looking defeated, but it only took a couple of encouraging words to lead him to rethink his decision and stick it out. I for one was glad he did, since he became an all-conference offensive tackle and one of the best players on the team.

Who on your team can use a word of encouragement today? So many stories are told about the amazing power of encouragement. Make it a daily habit to encourage everybody in your world.

**Success is in the little things you do
and in the things you say.**

COMPASSION

> Cum-Passio=to suffer with. Character, inner strength, responsible, empathy, excellent communicator and listener, generous, humility.

I can't help but think of Mother Teresa when I see the word *compassion*. Actually, Saint Teresa now. Her life is pretty well documented, and I recall her receiving the Nobel Peace Prize the year of my college graduation in 1979. She was actually canonized in September 2016. She didn't want this attention or prize, but she eventually agreed to accept it, and her speech was the prayer of Saint Francis: "Make me a channel of your peace." Her life *was* compassion. While in Calcutta, she actually put her life in danger "suffering with" the poor and desperate street people in the worst possible environment, including cholera, diarrhea, and malaria. She wasn't born a saint, she *became* a saint.

Recently I also watched a story on 60 minutes about a special school for kids who had Post Traumatic Stress Syndrome. Oprah Winfrey was the interviewer and she proclaimed this story profoundly changed her life, mainly because the counselors had uncommon compassion. Instead of asking the children what's wrong with them, they asked rather, what happened to you? The youngsters began to trust the counselors and tell their stories. What an amazing model and result.

In a similar way, as the leader of your team, it's sometimes necessary to put on the same uniform and work together on the front line, "suffering with" your people. Great leaders of the world, especially in the military, have done this. President Abraham Lincoln would fearlessly travel to a battlefield to meet with his generals face to face and compassionately walk amidst the wounded to give them empathy and hope.

Sometimes I think just a simple smile can make all the difference. We actually teach how to smile in our culture. If you can't smile, you can't work at Jersey Mike's. Well, at least on the front line. Maybe you can work the grill, since your back is toward the customer.

We know that research shows if you walk into a room with two people looking at you, one smiling and the other frowning, you immediately gravitate to the smiler. It's human nature and one of the universal laws of attraction. We have also found that when you smile, people tend to give you money (tips).

Researchers have found that empathy is the kindling that fires compassion, impelling us to help others. Further, even in adulthood, we can be trained to more kind and generous. So says Yudhijit Bhattacharjee, a contributing writer to *National Geographic*.

All Is Yours

When you come to me in need, I will certainly concede.
My ears are yours; please use them and proceed.
When you drop your "problem bomb,"
forget your shaky palm.
My hands are yours, grasping for your calm.
When you look at me upset, the moment eyes have met,
They are yours; no need to keep them wet.
When your soul knows only noise and logic thought destroys,
My mind is yours. I'll help to teach you poise.
When your heart outweighs your mind,
and its peace you seek to find,
My heart is yours, and your pain becomes mine.

LISTENING

To answer before listening, that is folly and shame.
—Proverbs 18:13
Let the wise listen and add to their learning.
—Proverbs 1:5

Create a listening culture. Get to know what your people are thinking. Solicit feedback from them. Make listening tangible. Learn by asking questions. In his book *The Coaching Habit*, Michael Stanier proposes seven important questions that a coach needs to ask. He proclaims we need to quiet the Advice Monster and respond through active listening after we ask the right questions. This is a unique method of coaching and effective when used correctly. The questions include the following:

- What's on your mind?
- And what else?
- What's the real challenge for you?
- What do you want?
- How can I help?

The important question for any business is, are you really listening to the answers? A good coach learns how to acknowledge the answer by paraphrasing or rephrasing what was said. For example: "I hear what you are saying is ___?" This can be practiced, especially with role-playing.

At the 2016 National Leadership Conference, Peter introduced keynote speaker Bill Marriott, who was celebrating his eighty-third birthday. Peter, having read Bill's latest book, *Spirit to Serve*, asked what he thought the greatest leadership skill was. Without hesitation, Bill answered, "Listening." He went on to say we need to ask our workforce, "What do you think?"

Peter understands this well and often proclaims how he himself had a voice working in the original Mike's Subs at age fourteen. The older guys would listen. When you study the art of listening, you quickly find that most people are not very good at it. This becomes a big opportunity for teaching and coaching. A coach who listens well, learns well.

One of the trickiest positions on the Jersey Mike's line is the sprinkler. These workers are required to intently listen to how our customers want their custom-made subs. Mike's Way (onions, lettuce, tomatoes, oil and vinegar, and spices) is our default and how we train all our crew, but in a loud and fast-paced atmosphere, intentional focus is required and needed to make every sandwich a sub above. We practice active listening and use training techniques like placing the extra item (pickle) on our sprinkle board when requested.

We also love teaching the art of remembering names. If you think you're not good at it, you're right. In fact, science shows us that the first step in remembering a name is simply telling your subconscious mind that you will. Next, use word association using a face or body part, like "Bill has brown hair" or "Nancy has a nice nose." You are halfway there when you use this technique. Dale Carnegie made a living teaching this. He said that a person's name is, to that person, the sweetest and most important sound in any language. There is great power in remembering names. It is definitely a skill that, when developed, can reap big rewards.

INSPIRATION

Enthusiasm—Greek="En-Theos" of the spirit, the Latin origin "in-spirare" or breathe into. How do you inspire someone? You breathe your spirit of enthusiasm into them.

In his book *Everyone Leads*, author Chris Lowney depicts bottom-up leadership for everyone. Everyone has the spirit inside. It's how the early Christians grew the church.

Here is a well-kept secret: You want to inspire your employees? Become an inspired leader. A community of monks taught me inspiration with their profound dedication to their beliefs. The quality of your thinking determines the quality of your life. The monks would challenge students with reflective questions like these:

- What books are you reading?
- Who are your friends?
- What do you watch on TV?
- What are you filling your mind with?

These things influence who you are and will become.

Choice not chance determines destiny.
—Aristotle

Choices makes the difference. Two people are in the same accident and severely wounded. They didn't choose to be in the accident. It just happened to them. But one of them chose to live the experience in bitterness, the other in gratitude. These choices radically influenced their lives and the lives of their families and friends. Good coaches teach their people to make prudent choices. That's how you can inspire.

Great teachers tell stories that bring drama. This makes people listen and learn better. There is a critical link between education and entertainment. In addition, research shows public praise has a great impact on others—this is from the book *Teach with Your Strengths: How Great Teachers Inspire Their Students*. As a former classroom teacher, I would also add that there is great benefit to working one-on-one whenever possible. Making a connection usually starts with wanting to inspire, which I believe is generated by love.

I've learned that people will forget what you said, people
will forget what you did, but people will
never forget how you made them feel.
—Maya Angelou

When you inspire people, they feel different. They see things differently, and they feel motivated to change their old ways and begin a new way. Sometimes a coach can do this in a group, but sometimes it takes some one-on-one attention.

As a manager, one of the greatest concerns is how to motivate employees to do their best work. You need to look to yourself and your enthusiasm for your position. Employees notice whether you have a genuine connection to your work. Modeling engagement with enthusiasm for your work is one of the best ways to inspire employees.

INTEGRITY

Success is having character in everything you do.

You may have heard that managers do things right, but leaders do the right thing. I like using the word *character* when thinking about integrity. If character is king, your word is your bond. A handshake seals a contract. You look someone in the eyes and tell them with firm handshake that the job will get done because you have integrity. It is a given.

Leading is a potent combination of strategy and character.
But if you must be without one, be without the strategy.
—General Norman Schwarzkopf

Character always trumps behavior. It's what you are versus
what you do. We need to navigate the business world carefully
today. Society seems to value winning at all costs. Contracts
mean nothing. Money lures many from another company or
team. Greed is good. Morality seems to be optional. It seems
we are willing to sacrifice character for conduct and integrity
for achievement.

The deeds you do may be the only sermon
some persons will hear today.
—Saint Francis of Assisi

The food business is hard and can be a three-headed
monster. The manager has huge responsibility for food safety,
great customer service, and hiring the right people. One misstep
and it's all over. Managers must develop into leaders if we are
going to be successful. They need navy SEAL–like training
before we commission them to lead others into this difficult
battle called the restaurant business. The number of failures
is usually linked to type and quality of training. According to
recent studies done by Professor Dr. H. G. Parsa, 59 percent of
hospitality facilities fail in the period of three years.

When I think of integrity, I also think about the word
faithful. Living a life of integrity requires telling the truth.
I have found honest, trustworthy people to have the
common denominator of being faithful people. A man of
character knows his limitations but refuses to accept them.

Success is being faithful, to your friends, your family, and your teammates throughout the years.

Today in our Jersey Mike's culture, Peter still operates with a handshake. He actually prefers that option.

DISCIPLINE

Without Discipline one cannot learn to be free.
—from "Cost of Discipleship" by Dietrich
Bonhoeffer, German theologian

When we think of discipline, we think of our ability to govern ourselves. The word comes from the Latin origin *discipulus*, meaning instruction or knowledge. It has the same root word as *disciple*, with its notion of surrendering ourselves to something or someone—like an athlete surrendering to the coach.

All athletes practice strict self-control. They do it to
win a prize that will fade away but we do it for an
external prize. So, run straight to the goal with purpose
in every step. I am not like the boxer who misses his
punches. I discipline my body like an athlete, training
it to do what it should. Otherwise, I fear that after
preaching to others I myself might be disqualified.
—Corinthians 9:25–27

Self-discipline is doing what needs to be done. Doing
it when it needs to be done. Doing it the best it can be
done and doing it that way every time you do it.
—Bobby Knight

Discipline develops strength of character in us, and character strengthens our confidence. I have found that the book of Proverbs is written to help us gain discipline for wise conflict management. It is my go-to for wise advice. It helps me develop a focused life.

Solomon himself said we should "love discipline" (Proverbs 12:1). As coaches, we need to demand it. We need not ask our people to try harder. We as coaches need, as the athlete knows, to train harder—physically, mentally, and spiritually. Jersey Mike's is a training company, and our trainers regularly attend coaching clinics to develop their skills.

Self-control gives us virtue, helping us to regulate our thoughts and emotions and choose between right and wrong in every part of our lives. It helps us to postpone immediate gratification. We need to battle for a disciplined life. The quality of your thinking determines the quality of your life, and if you want to improve your circumstances, you need to improve yourself.

I vividly recall one of my monk sessions concerning my legacy. Integrity was the word of focus. Character, conduct, actions, and attitudes were the words given to describe what will become a legacy—valuable words for a lifetime.

Two natures inside me
Fighting within,
One is love, the other sin.
Never certain which will win,
But the one I feed will proceed.

LOVE

> Love is the fruit in season at all times
> and within reach of every hand.
> —Saint Teresa

The monks gave me some parting gifts as I ventured into the real world, starting with eight magic words: *Everything you do must be done with love.* In addition, they gave me the new commandment: "Love one another."

When we are motivated by love, good things usually happen. It helps guide us on our pathway to sainthood, and it could be the greatest leadership concept on the planet. In my opinion, the biggest predictor of happiness and fulfillment overall in life is, basically, love. It seems to me, however, that our popular culture has a different meaning of what love is than what the monks taught. A little empathy, an effort to listen, kindness when you notice others are hurting—this is love!

The love we need here isn't a feeling. The Greeks gave us three types of love: *eros*, the romantic type like a husband and wife; *philos*, the brother love, as in Philadelphia, city of brotherly love; and *agape*, the unconditional love, the selfless love, the sacrificial love. It's that motherly love that is spiritual in nature.

Agape is the love we want in our stores. The stores that figure this out have a magic feeling inside their four walls. It usually translates to successful sales and service.

When Clemson defeated Alabama in 2017 for the national title in football, winning coach Dabo Sweeny was interviewed after the game on national TV. When asked about his words at halftime, he said he told his boys that he didn't know how they would win but they *would* win because of love. That's an amazing insight from a football coach, but it proved out, and the culture of love that he has cultivated continues to run through the veins of the players and coaches.

We need to intentionally use this word more in our lives: *I love the way you are wrapping that sub. I love how you sprinkled that sub. I really love how you talk to our customers. I love you, man.* We can say it, we can write it down, and we can act it out. What the world needs now ...

Success is when your loved ones seek only love from you.

His Love Is Where You Are

Be ready for your journey, for now it takes you far.
No worry for the future—His love is where you are.
His spirit dwells within you, no matter where you go.
The choice is yours; you'll make it well.
His wisdom now you know.
Your search is partly over. The treasure's in your heart,
Love is the key that opens doors—get ready then to start.
Prepare as does the teacher. Your heart the message tell,
And as the Shepherd tends his flock,
you'll tend your treasure well.

Ode to Him

If you could see inside of me,
This is what you'd find:
A humble and a contrite heart

Lying far beneath the mind.
The mind makes most decisions,
At least it thinks this way,
But often does consult the heart
To hear what it should say.
And if you could see inside of me,
You'd find a larger heart indeed,
And deep inside my heart,
You can tell apart
The dreams from the scars,
The darkness from the stars,
And deep inside, the words inscribed:
I love you
I **love** you
I love **you**.

———❀———

HUMILITY

Humility is one of those qualities that you really can't master.
The paradox is that once you think you have it, then you aren't
humble anymore. It's a lifelong discipline. We aren't born with
it. We're actually born totally self-dependent and self-centered.

Muhammad Ali's signature cry was "I am the greatest."
In reality, he led a humble life and figured the more he talked
about it, the less he'd become. He gave away a large amount
of his time, talent, and money during his lifetime. Most of the
great leaders in history know about humility and listening.

I've already mentioned monks and humility. Two of my
great lifelong mentors are monks: Father Dennis Meade and
Father Blaine Schultz. Combined, they have over a hundred

years of monastic wisdom. That's a lot of praying. I learned humility by their teaching but mostly by their lifestyle. I watched the way they walked the paths of life each day. They are not self-important or self-centered. Saint Benedict warned that would lead to a deformed soul.

The monks are known to be *meek*, an interesting word that actually means "strength under control." If that's the case, I'll aspire to be meek every day. Meek but not weak and strong in their faith are the monks. I'm always attracted to them and those with a humble spirit about themselves.

> For the Spirit does not make us timid, instead
> fills us with power, love and self-control.
> —2 Timothy 1:7

Coaches are made, not born. A coach without a well-thought-out plan will probably lose to a team that has a coach with these qualities. Every coach has a philosophy that systems are built from—certain goals and core values. Remember success is a team sport.

At an early age, I adopted the "7 Cs of Team Mentality." It was a foundation for a young coach to build from:

> communication
> collaboration
> commitment
> compassion
> consistency
> character
> caring

Team building is essential for any business and definitely part of our leadership plan at Jersey Mike's. Like the "7 Habits," the 7 Cs are a checklist for any aspiring coach to evaluate the goal at hand. Generally, my staff would come over on Sunday mornings after church for my famous pancakes and a coaches meeting. During the meeting, we would break down one of the Cs and discuss how to apply it to the team. It's always enjoyable and an effective way to mold the minds of the staff. A coach's clinic every Sunday. I'd miss those meetings in the off season.

THREE THINGS EVERY COACH MUST LEARN TO SAY

I'M SORRY

Coaches love to tell stories. Stories teach us some great lessons. In 1984, I was coaching at Washburn University, and we were preparing to play Mississippi Valley State. They were a feared team from the Southern conference and had several All-Americans. Jerry Rice was one of them. He would become the most prolific wide receiver in NFL history.

In his first several games of the season, he was averaging ten catches for 160 yards and averaging seventy-seven points a game. They had the first offensive line to average over three hundred pounds, nicknamed "Tons of Fun," and they hadn't run the ball once in their first three games. I was the defensive coordinator in charge of stopping this maniacal machine.

We actually had the lead at halftime with a minute left, but they were marching down the field, and my head coach, George Tardiff, called for a blitz. I didn't argue, but I didn't call the blitz either. The next play was the same.

The third play, the coach forced me to call the blitz, and you guessed it—Jerry Rice beat my man down the field and scored right before the half. I had to pay eighty dollars for the headset I threw on the ground (I had some maturing to do yet), and I ran to the locker room for halftime and kicked in a couple lockers before Coach Tardiff confronted me. He simply grabbed my shoulders, looked me in the eye, and said these words: "Keith, I'm sorry."

Wow. I was completely defused. I was an out-of-control maniac, and that simple phrase stopped me in my tracks. What a valuable lesson for me that day. I would learn to put it into use from that day forward, and I understand the power it still has today. Throw in "I apologize" and genuinely mean it, and you're back in the game.

THAT WAS MY MISTAKE

Everybody knows a leader learns to take the blame. When you admit and own up to a mistake, others see you aren't perfect, and since nobody is, maybe that's not such a bad idea.

As a young college assistant coach, I took my entire defensive squad to see the movie *Top Gun*. After all, we all had the need for speed! I bought everyone specially made Commando hats that had Blue Thunder on the front—our defense nickname.

The next day, much to my chagrin, the head coach called me into the office wondering why I was sabotaging the team. It was a big mistake on my part, and he was right. My intent was good, but I neglected the offensive squad. I had to make good on this mistake, and so I bought them hats with White Lightning on the front. A costly mistake in money and morale, but I learned a valuable lesson about what a team is. In the movie, Maverick needed Goose to fly the jet. Nobody is self-made.

THANK YOU

Another two-word powerhouse that, when used genuinely, can cause biochemical changes in the body, "thank you" reflects a grateful heart. It's a way of life. It cultivates happiness, contentment, and a positive attitude. It's one of the great universal laws of attraction. Even a "hey, thanks" with eye contact can make an impact and says you care. We have to make caring cool, and saying, writing, texting, or signing "thank you" can do that. When you express gratitude, you recognize that someone is valuable to you, and we hear this in our workplace every day. It's all about money. We all need to feel valued.

> Gratitude is not only the greatest of the
> virtues but the parent of all others.
> —Cicero

Cultivating gratitude doesn't cost money, but the benefits are enormous. Research shows improved physical health, psychological health, and sleep. Gratitude increases happiness, reduces depression, and enhances empathy. Gratitude increases mental strength. Also, recognizing all you have to be grateful for during the worst times of your life fosters resilience. Cultivating gratitude means focusing on what matters instead complaining about what you don't have. It's that old adage of "Better to want what you have than have what you want."

❚WHY WE WORK

There can be no joy in life without joy in work.
—Saint Thomas Aquinas

Everybody knows we all need money, and so we work. But we also know there are other reasons for working. When we travel the country asking our frontline crew members, they usually tell us there is a higher purpose in mind. In 2017, our operational word was *purpose*—the reason for which something is done.

What is your purpose? Is it managing? Is it becoming a better leader? Real purpose requires knowledge of the five Ps:

- purpose
- people
- product
- procedure
- profit

At Jersey Mike's, we say we are in the people business, and that means *people* are our *purpose*. Our brand ambassador, Coach John Hughes, has been teaching this concept for thirty-five years. That's more than five hundred classes. A great legacy, and he has been a mentor to many.

Our people are not a cost or expense but a valued commodity

that drives our business. We are so worried about profits and the bottom line that we put procedures in place geared toward getting our bonuses—not understanding the why. When we are obsessed with protecting the bottom line, we risk our *product* being compromised by cutting quality and amounts and letting machines do our work. We aim to practice sound *procedures* that explain why we do what we do.

Many companies have *profit* as their main purpose instead of people. When sales go down, they increase marketing, which increases cost, so they cut labor, which decreases morale. This diminishes the customer experience, which decreases sales, and we need more marketing. It is the vicious circle of doom.

At Jersey Mike's, we teach the opposite. If people are our purpose, then a great product, sound procedures, and high profits will come. Picture an employer who pays workers the bare minimum and refuses health insurance, paid vacation time, and other benefits. Such employers want profits, but lasting success can't be built on the backs of discontented, disloyal, overworked, underproductive employees. *Pay properly* would be two more Ps that apply to our franchisees. It's not enough just to have a positive goal. The goal needs to be in harmony with our thoughts and in line with appropriate wages.

One of our core missions is inspiring all our franchisees to pay their people well. We can't force them to do it, but our corporate store division practices what it preaches. The compensation package includes a performance-based bonus scale as well as a pay path that leads to ownership. Leaders take care of their people.

Peter has always preached that we are in the people business and that we are a training company. Our front line determines our bottom line. They need to be trained well. We call it our "fourteen feet of excellence and experience," and we invest in over one thousand training sessions annually, with specific initiatives handed down straight from the top. It's that sacred zone for us where we connect with our customers. Face-to-face isn't just a nice way to do business. "Our brains actually respond differently to in-person interactions," says Dr. Srini Pillay, an assistant clinical professor at Harvard Medical School. "Brain imaging research shows us that when people are in a face-to-face dialogue, this creates brain synchrony that results in a feeling of connection."

Our training programs always involve talking with our customers and sharing our lives with them. We refer to this as *bantering*. Our fourteen-foot counters are the perfect place for this. Generally, there are no phones or device distractions. People get serious when ordering their food. Those who master the art of bantering usually have high profits. Connecting with our customers is an integral piece of our training.

We believe that we are working for a bigger purpose. As Jon Gordon describes it in his book *The Seed*,

> When we find and live our purpose, it will provide the ultimate fuel for a meaningful life. You may not build libraries around the world but you can find the bigger purpose in reading to your children. You may not feed the homeless every day but you can nourish your employees and customers with a smile, kind word and care. And while you may not start your own non-profit organizations you can begin a charity initiative at work. After all, "charity" means "love in action." You can make a difference every day and touch the lives of everyone you meet.

Rick Warren, in his best-seller *The Purpose-Driven Life*, says that when we understand our purpose in life, food tastes better and music sounds better. We tap into a supernatural source that just makes life better.

We generally close our leadership class in New Jersey with this final statement:

> A customer is the most important visitor on our premises. He is not dependent on us. We are dependent on him. He is not an interruption in our work. He is the purpose of it. He is not an outsider in our business. He is part of it. We are not doing him a favor by serving him. He is doing us a favor by giving us an opportunity to do so.

Our ops word for year 2018 is *focus*—all-hands-on-deck type of focus, not-taking-things-for granted focus. Keeping up record sales and service because we are teaching focus. The focus is on our customers; we understand who really pays our salaries.

Thank you, Jon Gordon, for inspiring us with the *One Word* book you published back in 2013. We immediately adopted it, and it has produced several great words for our company culture, such as *elevate, inspire, relentless, urgency,* and *purpose.*

But here's the problem: research is telling us that very few people are happy at work. Most studies are showing upwards of 70 percent unhappy—one foot out the door. "The quit before they quit." A virtual nationwide workforce of "puddle glums," a favorite term of C. S. Lewis. Here's what we have found out: Employees don't leave their jobs. Employees leave their managers! And when they leave, it's costly, financially and emotionally. Cornell University's Center for Hospitality Research estimates that it costs businesses $5,864 for every employee lost, and $15,000 for a lost manager. It's hard to measure the emotional stress this creates, but often lost managers will try to steal employees away.

Our modern workplace seems disconnected—emotionally alone, isolated, exhausted, anxious, and worried. Employees are worried about disapproval, looking stupid, and poor results. The end result is underachieving.

We need to get our people connected to their coworkers and the company mission statement. Getting them excited about contributing helps them understand the concept of team. If we foster the type of environment where it's safe for employees to be themselves, we can inspire them to do more than they thought possible. It's back to team spirit, and that requires a head coach capable of understanding the dynamics of the culture. Coaches need to spend quality time with their A players, being careful not to praise their ability but their effort. Focus on persistence and *grit*—a great word and great character trait.

Work is Love made Visible.
—Kahlil Gibran

Time magazine produced a special study on how joy affects health and what determines happiness. The results suggest that 50 percent of our propensity for happiness is inherited. Further, 40 percent of our ability to be happy is governed by our own choices, such as exercising and socializing. The smallest influence is external circumstances, like beauty and income, at 10 percent. Clearly, we have a lot to do with our own happiness.

The Dalai Lama said this: "In my own limited experience, the basic source of all happiness is love and compassion, a sense of kindness and warm-heartedness toward others. When we are calm and relaxed we can make proper use of our mind's ability to think clearly, so whatever we do, whether we are studying or working, we will be able to do it better. People respond positively to kindness." At Jersey Mike's, we have a special formula for creating happy crew members: if you want to be happy you have to get holy, and the way to get holy is to get serving!

Saint Paul called the early believers a community of saints. Pope Francis encourages all of us to be saints. The book *Pathway to Sainthood* says, "You may not be one but you could be but you'll never be unless you believe you can be." A trash collector can become a saint. Holiness isn't reserved for monks and nuns. It does not mean goody-goody; it means *set apart for sacred use.*

We have to rethink what we're doing. Simply doing what you are told at work is not the stuff of saints. We must find creative, hidden, and effective ways to serve others at work and at home, going beyond the call of duty and sacrificing to the point where it begins to hurt. Everyone is called to a holy life, *especially* in the workplace.

The "divine command" expressed by Pope Francis is that we are born to work. We are designed to socialize with groups. We need to teach and coach this to our crew members. Working hard is virtuous and can be holy. The Jersey Mike's franchise model teaches the franchisee to "suffer with" our crew members serving our customers side by side on our front lines. They are constantly coaching the message that "our purpose is the customer."

Serving—that's the final piece of the formula. If you want to be happy, you gotta get holy, and you get holy by serving. Servant leadership is not just a phrase for us. Our teaching in the stores incorporates holding a door open and observing in our lobbies to assist with filling a drink, grabbing extra trash, or wiping off a table or chair. Many of our younger workforce have never held a door open or a seat for someone before. Our crews eventually learn that manners and old-school hospitality matter. I still occasionally hum the old number one song of the year from 1979 by Robert Zimmerman, a.k.a. Bob Dylan: "Gotta Serve Somebody." Good reminder for us all. I believe happiness leads to success, not the other way around.

> Anyone can be great because anyone can serve. You only need a heart full of grace, a soul generated by love.
> —Martin Luther King Jr.

The Holy Question

If there never was a question, then how would we respond?
Maybe the question would cause us to shut up for a second.
The proper answer is to listen.
The question might tell us how to respond.
And what if we don't respond to the question?
Should we have another question?
Should we not understand the question in order to answer it?
How could we respond to a question if
we don't know enough about it?
And what if we should respond incorrectly?
My question for you is this: Is there a question in your life?
If not, who then answers yours?

HABITS

"Wax on, wax off." People remember this phrase and action from Mr. Miagi in the movie *The Karate Kid*. At one point, he also gives the advice, "Miagi say no try. Just do!" The karate kid has to do this mind-numbing work over and over again. He creates a habit.

> We are what we repeatedly do, excellence
> therefore is not an act but a habit.
> —Aristotle

Working in a Jersey Mike's store is a daily mind-numbing exercise of disciplined habits. Every morning is the same: Slice the onions to the exact spec. Slice the lettuce to the exact spec. Slice the tomato (red, ripe, and ready) to the exact spec. Prepare the bread and bacon and prepare for the lunch rush. Every day, 362 days a year.

In the movie *Rocky*, Apollo Creed tells the Italian Stallion that he's going to drop him like a bad habit. Actually, getting rid of a bad habit is a very difficult thing to do. Our lives are a series of habitual events. We seem to live almost unconsciously throughout the day as we go from habit to habit. Scientists argue how many days it takes to make or break a habit, but I don't think that matters. I have learned through my experience as a life coach that to break a habit one must develop a personal list of coping strategies that can replace the old habit.

For example, consider the urge to eat ice cream. Instead of eating it, you replace that behavior with walking the dog, reading a book, or eating yogurt. You develop a predesigned meaningful list of behaviors that are not self-defeating. Now you have a shot at dropping the habit. I once had a crew member at Jersey Mike's who repeatedly would bark out "My bad" while working lunch. This was a behavior that was unacceptable behind the line and in front of customers. When those words came close to coming out, he learned to replace them with "Pardon me." It took a while, but the habit was eventually broken.

One of the most popular business books on the planet is Steven Covey's *7 Habits of Highly Effective People*. We have adopted these habits, and for years our operations and training team has attempted to live them. As one of their leaders, I have embraced the habits myself and enjoy teaching them regularly. I was amazed recently during a visit to my daughter's second-grade classroom where she teaches the habits through a special program for inner-city kids. I was more amazed that they could recite all seven. What an encouraging thing to see. They actually learned to sing them.

But Covey had another book that followed: *First Things First*. It is an equally amazing read, more than four hundred pages chock-full of concepts that are clearly supported by scripture. He describes frustration using word pictures of a clock and a compass. The clock represents commitments, schedules, time, and appointments. The compass is our vision, our mission in life, and important things. The problem, it seems, is that there is a huge gap between them.

We need to teach ourselves how to put first things first in our lives before we can teach others. Many books have piggybacked on this notion, but Covey's first and most important question to us is, "What one activity has the most significant positive result in your life?" As a life coach, my milk and meat in the morning is reading God's inspired word, and I thank the monks once again for that.

The compass tells us where to go, but the gap exists because of the clock that seems to betray us. We know what to do, but we don't do it because we're spread too thin or the job is too big or we just can't find the time. This gap will only close when we learn about another tough word: discipline. It's the challenge of change, and I think it starts with another habit, and that is the habit of balance. I believe it can lead us to a purposeful, godly life that ultimately leads us to happiness.

The Balance

I sometimes wonder if I should do more than I do now.
Many gifts have blessed me, but can I do more and how?
To redefine my world of work, I must find a place for peace.
Stress becomes the lingering disease
and forbids the work to cease.
If I'm at all intelligent, then I pray the Lord will give
The right amount of energy to balance how I live.

TIPS FOR NURTURING YOUR MIND, BODY, AND SPIRIT

In 1984/85, I had the great pleasure to work with the Fellowship of Christian Athletes. Bones Nay was the regional director. I joined forces with head coach Bill McCartney of the Colorado Buffaloes, and in the off-season we went on a speaker's tour of the Midwest, inspiring athletes. My message was entitled the Three-Dimensional Athlete, and it focused on balancing mind, body, and spirit. What the mind conceives, the body achieves.

I was raised to believe the body is a temple, a sacred vessel that we need to nurture and treat with respect. Years later, I would add a piece about the heart, the emotional dimension that includes conversations about love. Coach McCartney would win a national championship in 1990 and go on to start Promise Keepers Men's Ministries. His rallies would fill the same stadiums that he coached in.

Over the years, I have developed the following tips for nurturing your mind, body, and spirit, drawing heavily from lessons I learned from the monks:

- *Learn to slow down.* Carve out time to discern where to put your energy. Some forms of busyness don't serve us well. The wise Trappist monk Thomas Merton recognized the effects of getting too caught up in projects and trying to help everybody. Sometimes we need to just say no.
- *Shut the phone off.* We all know the amazing addictive powers of the cell phone. We now have a generation of children actually addicted to their devices, and we really don't know the long-term consequences. At least set some guidelines.

- *Work out.* Get moving! Whatever turns you on turns on endorphins, which we need to feel good. Connecting with our bodies is essential for long-term health. Even thirty minutes can make a difference. Just be consistent. Create the habit. As Henry David Thoreau wrote, "Every man is the builder of a temple called his body. We are all sculptors and painters, and our material is our own flesh and blood and bones. Any nobleness begins at once to refine a man's features, any meanness or sensuality to imbrute them."

- *Get outside.* Reconnecting with nature is where we belong. In his book *Natural Born Heroes*, Christopher McDougall cites research on how much more enhanced our lives are with time spent outside. Some cultures that spend lots of time outside have developed their senses to incredible levels. We're designed to be outdoor creatures, not stuck in a chair looking at a screen all day. One of my favorite inspirations is getting up early to watch the sunrise and walking down the beach barefoot. It tends to be a glorious event.

- *Cultivate relationships.* Quality time is having a cup of coffee with an old friend. How about a call or text to tell someone how valuable they are to you—family, friends, coworkers. No one ever says on their deathbed that they wish they'd spent more time at work. I personally block off an hour every weekend just to make calls to those people I love and need to keep connected to.

- *Know your God.* I think when we neglect our spiritual natures, we miss out on a big piece of who we are. Use whatever gets you to transcendence—meditation, reading, writing, looking at art. The monks always reminded us athletes not to forget our spiritual muscles.

REFLECT, RECONNECT, AND CULTIVATE

It all starts with being mindful of what matters to us in life. The quality of our thinking reflects the quality of our lives. We get to choose.

Burnout rates in restaurants are notoriously high. Peter designed our franchise model with this in mind. An owner/operator would work Monday through Friday, half a day Saturday, and be off on Sunday. That's balance, and that's an attractive business model, which is one big reason franchisees are seeking us out. Leaders take care of their people with reasonable scheduling and compensation.

Danny Malamis, franchisee and Jersey Mike's area director, puts his money where his mouth is. Twice annually, he plans a weekend retreat for his management team. The format reminds me of the monks. A little company culture, a little quiet reflection, and whole lotta sharing of ideas and deeper thoughts. What a great way to build trust and genuine friendship.

This investment in people is the example that leads the way to success. I would suggest that learning balance is a key habit that will lead to a happier life. Many moons ago during my early coaching career, I picked up this poem, which I've used throughout this book. It's forever etched in my memory:

Success is in the way you walk the paths of life each day.
It's in the little things you do, and in the things you say.
It's not in reaching heights or fame.
It's not in only reaching goals that most all seek to claim.
Success is being big of heart not measured by your peers.
It's being faithful to your family, your friends, and your teammates through the years.

Success is when your loved ones seek only love from you.
Success is having character in everything you do.

—unknown

As part of our culture, our Jersey Mike's corporate-office employees are required to complete what we call our in-store experience. This allows for an actual glimpse of what's is like to work the line in our stores. The shift is a full day, and the following emails are a typical example of why we do this:

> **From:** Shawn Giles
> **Sent:** Friday, December 01, 2017 4:16 PM
> **Subject:** My In-Store Experience
>
> Hello Mr. Hertling,
>
> I had the privilege of working a day at the Red Bank store (1044). I rubbed elbows with some of the up-and-coming JM employees. I spent most of the day behind the register chatting up customers as they waited and paid for their food. You can really feel the strain for time when the line gets long. It is helpful to remember this experience when on the phone. I have personally worked in a fast-paced food environment before, but it was still good to see members of the staff remain a sub above even in the tightest of times. It's important to see the same camaraderie and teamwork we use on the Help Desk at the store level. Our job does not get done without the people around us, and it was the same at the store.

From: Laurie Guinan
Sent: Tuesday, November 21, 2017 9:43 AM
To: Keith Hertling
Subject: In-Store experience

Good Morning, Mr. Hertling!!

At the risk of being accused of "brown-nosing"—
Yesterday, I had my first in-store experience at
the Red Bank Store. I feel compelled to share
my experience in hopes that they get some
kudos!! I was so nervous when I got there but
immediately, Joe, Jimmy, Andrew, and Kevin
all made me feel right at home. Each one of
them took the time to teach me how things are
done and there was always one of them right
next to me while I was working the register to
make sure I was doing ok. It really was a great
experience and a really nice, sincere bunch of
guys! I have worked in restaurants and delis
over the years, and I have never seen a cleaner,
more organized store! No doubt that is the JM
standard, but to actually see it was impressive! I
was trying to keep busy while it was slow, and
the "Mom" in me wanted to clean, but there
wasn't much to tackle. LOVE IT!

From: Kristin Loriot
Sent: Wednesday, December 13, 2017 1:36 PM
Subject: In store experience

Keith,

I was the first of the Help Desk to get thrown into the store experience and it was such a delight! I went to store 1010 in Howell, and it was a really eye-opening experience to see the tasks they have to perform in their day-to-day. The team worked together very well once the rush came, and I did some register ringing throughout the lunch rush. This gave me some perspective on how to keep up with ringing and remaining professional, polite, and calm while the line built up. There were a handful of regulars that the staff all knew, and you can tell the customers really appreciated the Jersey Mike's experience in Howell. I took some time toward the end of the shift to sit aside with Kyle to pick his brain on his labor management techniques with his employees for CrunchTime! purposes. Working with Kyle was beneficial because he was able to give us insight into how they manage their CT while running the store.

|FINAL COACHING THOUGHTS

Everybody knows you have to coach your people. I suggest that coaching is not a profession but a mind-set, a way of being. Yes, you will schedule a session at a certain time, but it's not about that. A sub-above coach will coach all the time and whenever necessary. The coaching moment occurs when we least expect it. With 360-degree vision, we see when it's necessary to intervene and provide a certain pearl of wisdom or make an adjustment.

I'm not a psychiatrist, but I have a couple of friends who are, and they tell me that people don't change. I can't argue the matter; there's no debating it. They are very righteous in that people don't change *unless* they want to. I personally agree.

One of my favorite coaches I worked with in my coaching career was hall-of-fame coach Roy Williams when he was at Kansas University. He had great insight into his players, and one of his favorite slogans was "you've got to have *want-to.*" Change only happens when you get that player/person to want to change.

Think differently. That's the coaching challenge. When you possess the coaching qualities described in this book, I think you have a greater chance of getting someone to think differently and eventually act differently.

Psychologists agree that you can't change behavior while you continue to think the same thoughts that brought you to where you are. The definition of insanity given to us by Albert Einstein is "doing the same thing over and over again and expecting different results." To improve your circumstances, you need to improve yourself. Self-discipline is the key to obtaining anything you want. Great leaders learn how to create the *want* and teach the *how*, which answers the *why*.

LEADERS ARE LEARNERS

Wise men and women are always learning,
always listening for fresh insights.
—Proverbs 18:15

Dov Seidman, author of *Why How We Do Anything Means Everything*, makes a case that you can change behavior but only through relationships and morality. He says in order to inspire, you have to walk the talk. He loves to talk about moral leadership. Leaders who are driven by purpose elevate others. We know what we can and cannot do. Moral leaders do what they should do. I think this leads to empowerment and trust. Peter Cancro is such a leader, and he was bred on doing the right thing.

The monks would refer to this moral clarity as fortitude, one of the four cardinal virtues. The monks always taught that we are here to make the world better. The least we can do is focus on making things better for our families and those in our workplaces. Those of us in our sub shops ... well, you can't be a sub above if you don't leave your world in a better place. Growing up in my neighborhood, we were raised to help others, not wait to be helped. We can do this by focusing on our customers and making sure they leave happier than when they came in. It's the Golden Rule.

The coach's creed, the champion not fully satisfied, and playing until the whistle blows were three life lessons that led to what a sub above is today. At Jersey Mike's, we aren't waiting. We believe the time to give is now. The time to make a difference is at hand:

- Help nourish.
- Help flourish.
- Be a sub above.

When potential new franchisees and outsiders investigate our culture, they are usually quite surprised and in disbelief. This is mainly because Peter literally handpicked every employee in our company. It's what he did when he first hired his early staff. Actually, he really never hired in the traditional sense; rather, he would recruit the sharpest kids in line who he'd been observing, and when the time was right, Peter simply asked when they could start working with his team. It was all organic.

This system today I don't believe is matched anywhere in the business universe. Referencing Steven Covey's habit number 2, "Begin with the end in mind," Peter visualized what his company could become. The kids he hired at fourteen and fifteen years of age were raised on the product and his leadership, both still unmatched today. There would be no sacrificing quality of product or quality of people.

Everywhere we go, people remark on how Peter has surrounded himself with great people. These were the brothers and sisters of loyal friends and family who genuinely vested themselves in the mission. Some went to college, but many did not. The names listed below are but a sampling of seasoned warriors who started early and now are in leadership roles with our company. All worked behind the counter and all lived our authentic culture, and still do. Jersey Mike's was the first job for almost all on this list:

- Brenda Bates, area director, franchisee, and lifetime achievement award recipient
- John Hughes, brand ambassador, thirty-five years
- Dave Altmann, special operations
- Josh Funderburk, director of training
- Evan Mayer, codirector of operations with Rob Cancro
- Steve Capestro, special projects
- Brian Loughran, regional vice president/operations
- Marco Panicali, regional vice president/operations
- Chris Daniels, regional vice president/operations
- Kevin Loughran, corporate store director
- Mitch Thomson, northeast area director
- Chad Tirpack, director of compliance/training
- Pat Tighe, field representative
- Al Graziano, field representative
- Jen Fioretti, field representative
- Evan Ventura, field representative
- Cody Waldron, field representative

This partial list is a reflection of our entire office. Everyone bleeds oil and vinegar.

Last but not least is COO Mike Manzo, who started with Peter in high school before he joined the marines and then returned to the business after serving his country. He has never stopped serving and never will. I refer to him often as our CCO, chief *caring* officer. He is truly an officer and a gentleman—and Peter's right hand for nearly forty years.

These dedicated and valued saints were personally selected by Peter based on their character and the qualities described in this book. Our turnover is small, but our results have been big. Peter Cancro is a man on a mission. He has assembled a lifetime of servant leaders all understanding what our simple mission has been since 1975: *giving*. We are making a difference in the lives of others.

The following index cards are the originals from my college years, 1975–79. They are time-tested pearls of wisdom. Please enjoy.

Mark Twain on "Fun"

"Fun is what you do when you
don't have to do it"

Those who want to leave an impression for one
year should plant corn.

Those who want to leave an impression for 10
years should plant a tree.

Those who want to leave an impression for 100
years should educate a human being.
— Chinese Proverb

Discipline is always
in all ways.

Better to want what you have
than to have what you want.
Live an attitude of gratitude.
You are not what you think you
are, but what you think — you are!
Choose not choose Victoria's
destiny.

As long as there is an open mind,
there will always be a frontier.

If you fail to plan.
If you plan to Fail!

If necessity is the mother of
invention, then boredom is the mother
of creativity.

You cannot push anyone up the
ladder unless he is willing to
climb himself.
— Andrew Carnegie

Put on board "Motto of the Week"

"Communication is the key to Success"
— Conway Hall
— Oliver

Word of the Week

Motivation

Forum:

"destination"

The most valuable of all talents is that
of never using two words when one will do.
— Thomas Jefferson

You teach best what you most
need to learn.

Great spirits have always
encountered violent opposition
from mediocre minds.
— Einstein

If I can supply you with a thought,
You may remember it or you may not.
But if I can make you think a thought
for yourself, I have indeed added to your
stature. *Elbert Hubbard*

Life is no 'brief candle' for me. It is a sort
of splendid torch which I have got hold of
for a moment, and I want to make it burn as
brightly as possible before handing it on to
future generations.
George Bernard Shaw

When one door closes, another opens;
but we often look so long and so
regretfully upon the closed door that we do
not see the one which has opened for us.
Alexander Graham Bell

Practice does not make perfect;
perfect practice makes perfect.
Vince Lombardi

Give me a fish and I eat for a day,
Teach me to fish and I eat for a lifetime.

If you're not part of the solution
you're part of the problem.

Original Popeye's Gym circa 1971

Point Pleasant Beach Garnet Gulls, 1975, "The Big 4": 42—Chip Sherman, 43—Peter Cancro, 44—Keith Hertling, 33—Tom Spiegel

Keith with monk mentor Father Dennis Meade, 2015

Jersey Mike's Tough Mudder Team, 2015

‖APPENDIX

SPECIAL OLYMPICS

Faces, braces, different places, these weekends special times.
Glowing, growing, people showing just how much these events
mean to them.
Special smiles, special people, Special Olympics—
To measure the pleasure found here would be impossible.

Straying, playing, even praying,
Praying for simple things
Like love and faithful friends, for friends who show they care.

Dancing, chancing, definitely romancing,
Most of these kids have no walls,
No barriers to hold them back, except society.
We glare and stare at these kids,
Not always in a caring way,
Sometimes thinking, Who gives them the right to be here?
Who gives it to you?

Special Olympics is hope for these kids.
Hope to leave the house a while,
Hope to dance the night away,
Hope to meet other special people,

Hope to be somebody.
Hope to see you at the next Special Olympics.

TO FINALLY BECOME NO ONE

Of course I seek attention,
And I know I've been well-known,
And there can be no denying
Through the years my star has shone.
But it's been my understanding,
If you want to be a star,
You got to scrape off all the glitter
And be the one you truly are.

Well I've had my time in glory,
And I live my life the most,
But my life's a whole new story,
And there ain't no time to boast.
You know stars shine just in darkness,
And that ain't no place to be.
We gotta live our lives together
And become what we should be.

Now I've seen some complications,
And it's made some people sad.
Only time becomes the master
Of the things I could have had.
If you want to be somebody,
Then do what the wise men say:
Just live your life like Jesus,
And you'll be famous on that day.

DESTINY

Yes, it is predestined, but life must still be planned,
For if you don't outline your ways, you're like a ship unmanned.
Since I believe that life goes on even after death,
I choose to live my life as if each day is my last breath.
My God blessed me with this life, and I try to live it well,
So when my time is up on earth, my book will clearly sell.
Each day becomes a life for me, each hour like a year,
And as I hope and pray each day, my life becomes more clear.
Yes, heaven is the destiny, my dream, my fairy tale,
And if I fail to plan it now, for sure I'll plan to fail.

MORE THAN A GAME

When you're getting ready for battle
And conditions cause you to sweat,
Remember what teachers once told you:
You'll perform as prepared as you get.
So be sure to get yourself ready.
We all know just what it takes.
Some do respond to the challenge,
Some don't and blame it on breaks.
So attack every task that confronts you.
Be alert and sharp as a knife.
Keep your head up, and always remember
It's a game, but the game is called life.

DON'T CRITICIZE

Have you ever wondered why some kids hate?
Perhaps they can't communicate.
Perhaps there's a message in their wild outcries,
But no matter how wild, stay calm and mild, show love to that child.
Don't criticize.

Kids can be fragile from the time of their birth,
Starting from childhood, they learn of their worth.
If you want them all healthy, then tell them no lies.
Tell them how much, show them by touch, let love be the crutch.
Don't criticize.

I have not seen yet a child who will bloom
If for every mistake, he was sent to his room.
If you want them to grow, then see through their eyes,
And no matter how old, be wise as you scold, treat them like gold.
Don't criticize.

Some kids will do whatever they can,
But sometimes we fail to understand.
Not to listen would be very unwise.
Show them you care, be firm and be fair, you may pull out your hair, but
Don't criticize.

Personalities change through the years as they raise,
Success seems to breed with the usage of praise,
Some kids reject it, but it's just a disguise.

Don't be a fool, use praise as your tool, let love be the rule.
Don't criticize.

Their minds need our guidance throughout as they grow.
The models we use in return they will show.
A change in behavior may be no surprise.
What can we give for love to live? Be positive.
Don't criticize!

NOW

We seldom see the leaves turn;
Our focus much within.
We rarely feel the heart yearn;
Instead, we live the sin.

What does it take to see then
How much there really is?
When will we ever realize
That everything is His?

Lord, please keep us mindful.
You're so close in many ways.
See that we are careful
Not to miss you any days.

I'll share the love you give me,
Not always knowing how.
I'll seek to see your turning leaves
And live the moment now.

CPSIA information can be obtained
at www.ICGtesting.com
Printed in the USA
BVHW091140260421
605876BV00013B/244